Rare Sighting of a Guillotine on the Savannah

Rare Sighting of a Guillotine on the Savannah

Michael Trussler

Mansfield Press

Printed in Canada

Library and Archives Canada Cataloguing in Publication

Title: Rare sighting of a guillotine on the savannah / Michael Trussler.
Names: Trussler, Michael, 1960- author.
Description: Poems.
Identifiers: Canadiana 2021034038X | ISBN 9781771262743 (softcover)
Classification: LCC PS8639.R89 R37 2021 | DDC C811/.6—dc23

Cover Image: Cy Twombly, *The Four Seasons: Summer*
Author Photo: Amy Snider
Editor: Jim Johnstone
Layout & Design: Erica Smith

ONTARIO ARTS COUNCIL
CONSEIL DES ARTS DE L'ONTARIO
an Ontario government agency
un organisme du gouvernement de l'Ontario

Canada Council for the Arts
Conseil des arts du Canada

The publication of *Rare Sighting of a Guillotine on the Savannah* has been generously supported by the Canada Council for the Arts and the Ontario Arts Council.

Mansfield Press Inc.
25 Mansfield Avenue, Toronto, Ontario, Canada M6J 2A9
Publisher: Denis De Klerck
www.mansfieldpress.net

"Drifting over the earth, we encounter a crystallization of parrot-event and glacier-event, each of them defining a fateful tear in the contexture of meaning, the birth of an individual power to be reckoned with."

Graham Harman, *Tool-Being*

"Allegorical writing is a writing of its time, saying slant what cannot be said directly, usually because of overtly political regimes of the sacred nature of the message."

Vanessa Place and Robert Fitterman, *Notes on Conceptualisms*

Table of Contents

Zen and a Dinosaur

Three Minds

Self-Portrait

Look into a mirror for a while.

A shark is floating in formaldehyde behind you.
Exhale into the glass that's keeping your face. Look at

the mark on the mirror breathing makes. How
it obscures and distorts everything. Makes
evidence
to the contrary. Early this morning, dammit, I couldn't
see quite right.

Does anyone know what time it is?

Children and parents and other kinds
of people are kept waiting—
                                        The twentieth century was hand-
crafted in Berlin, began choking, and then limped
to New York City, where it spun around exactly twice, a drunken
Icarus, before falling down the collapsing
stairs—

Harmony
        and its twin:
                              brutality: both stretched so far they
open up a space for other
sounds to occupy—

Too much flame.

And what if what I want most is for you to want most what I'd most
like to receive?

Look into your favourite
mirror. Tie a snake to each wrist. An aging
                                                            surrealist, A, B
                                                            see
all the way to morning   a shark
is waiting in formaldehyde in front of you, it sounds

from there to here. From me to you. From
everywhere—trying to undo
what's been found
mnemonic and incessant and incomplete.

My Single Lifetime in Exchange for a Burst

"Man is the only animal that shoots other creatures with paintball guns, and when the creatures flap around in terror or fall to the ground injured and in shock, man is the only animal that cheers."

Deborah Bird Rose, "Shimmer: When all You Love is Being Trashed"

of your attention   once more   My Single Lifetime in Exchange
for a Burst of your attention   says everybody   says
the dead utterly attentive entrepreneur   so here's some restorative
design   Earth to Bauhaus Bauhaus to Earth *come in*
come in   but nobody answers even today so   breathe on these
very words right now   and look   your breath makes a grey fog
and these lines they   in turn   diagnose the denial that's chronic
inside your chest   our breathing
eventually becoming biodegradable
                                                            it's a hassle and fun's fun but isn't
anyone gonna pick up the Goddamn ball offers
the dead entrepreneur   Look around   waking up these days is

     so scattered   waking up

these days is like *have you ever left*
something you need   *left it in a taxi* ... what we
need   we need what's offered

in an ocelot's curious gaze   gets
                                                            (A work of art is like a transparent bag
                                                             full of eyes,
and each eye is also a transparent bag full of eyes—Timothy Morton)   gets
what's outside of what's suddenly

here   Listen   *if you want one ambulance or*
dialysis machine, you must accept a militarised world full of poisoned
rivers, mediocre livelihoods, toxic oceans, dead soil and an
atmosphere full of greenhouse gases and pollution   this is a found

poem we=each=have=become=a=found=poem *This is a hard reality*

for anyone—such as myself—who has had a loved one 'saved' by
industrial medicines or technologies to accept, but one that we
must address if we're not going to inflict future generations

(for David Buckel)

with all the same physical and psychological
diseases of our toxic
culture—
Mark Boyle, who's been *Drinking Molotov Cocktails with Gandhi*

and blessed

are and blessed are
the indifferent who shall

Nina from Beirut Stamps Her Foot

And claps her hands to tell the back yard koi
their food is floating right in front of them.

She's 7, but I'd guessed older. She told me
she's flown this summer from Beirut to Spain

to Paris to Halifax and now to Regina where
we're at her famous grandfather's wake in

front of the koi. And yes, she speaks French,
a little Arabic, and why won't they take their

food she asks, not really to anyone
here in Regina. *Auspicious ... yanked* and

acolyte are golden yet tattered words I've not
used in decades. I met them while reading

this morning, so add them to my missing
words list in a moleskin diary and in front

of the koi begin counting back from one
hundred in sevens to chart my disappearing

brain. Apoptosis. Do you see that hammered
man vaping over there? That's what addiction's

suddenly come to. Being an adult is sometimes
like pounding a telescope face down

like a spike, down into the earth,
I decide against telling her,

Nina who's seven, who's leaving tomorrow
for Toronto and Halifax, then Spain and Paris

and finally back home to pretty Beirut again,
leaving her grandfather who joked so well, who

fashioned his own urn one day at the wheel daring his
old friend—some porcelain—to see if it could hold him.

Three Minds

1.

One behind binoculars watching this morning's unknowable
heron-in-the-reeds swallowing
                                        a fish ↔ its brain alight with unassailable
suffocation—   Life's dark velocity and it's suddenly autumn—

And then munching grapes in bed, grapes shipped from Peru, and watching
a military crew setting off to explore the windy compound in the movie
Aliens, our eight-year-old son quietly says: climate change is certainly going
to be worse than this—

                                        And yesterday, my friend who's younger than me
                                        and writes essays
                                                    on troubled Japanese avant-garde
                                                    photographers

leans suddenly through a doorway
holding an ebony cane,
smiling across the pitch dark, a looming synapse
inhabiting the best light-macabre
money can buy, and each of us   and each of us all
                                        we've met in some unraveling

rainy and deserted place we've never known and something rises up
and speaks to us from the vast length of what's finite   and what's
mute, and what's incredibly been left behind—

The mind is a body surprised by space.

2.

Troubled because what can ever be done? 1 + 1 + 1 > the past
as a perplexed eye

I once imagined
that trying to imagine someone else's loss
was like trying to carve something out of a waterfall.

And that's the moment to decide what exactly
you want to do   with what remains of
the rest of your life.

What's claustrophobic, what's rioting
inside what's about to happen:
inside these neural circuits our brains fire

as bright as the nocturnal
seeds of a pomegranate newly opened. Elsewhere—

and gone: the wars of the samurai
in the unspent sixteenth century,
in which many thousands of women
lost their husbands and sons,
sometimes (it's said) sometimes
these wars caused strange and tragic
complications—

Life's velocity. He'd only taken LSD
a few X, but that was decades ago ...
and once he saw a burst of harmless
perfection: a line of tiny-neon-green
cacti receding beyond an eternity
stretching from his very fingertips.

Winter is iccumin in. Lude sing
Goddamn

Now

with Rothko Chapel playing in one   ear and a new winter storm
in the other ↔ both pressing   down on last week's touch

of spring ↔ both calling   to each other as if I'm not
here and most likely   I'm not the sleet in the wind

this morning's eyelid closing   over a songbird though not
the one that impales its prey   on thorns and then stores

its food there to feed its young   the great grey shrike
how could something like this   have begun to happen

today's the last day for Agnes Martin   in Saskatchewan   outside
and leaf-side everything's always   leaving   a waiter enters left

carrying   a tray   it's Santos   the ghost of Santos
the waiter from Texas   back from when we were single

and scrubbing ourselves down   to our constituent thoughts
it takes the elegance of time   so much time to build

the back yard shed where a life's   difficult-to-calculate failures
can be hung up to dry   there's no defense against
the laziness born from rejection   I don't deserve it but never

have I felt so rescued

After the Night Rain ...

After the Night Rain

"Only when in technology body and image so penetrate that all revolutionary tension becomes bodily collective innervation and all the bodily innervations of the collective become revolutionary discharge, has reality transcended itself to the extent demanded by the Communist Manifesto. For the moment, only the Surrealists have understood its present commands. They exchange, to a man [sic], the play of human features for the face of an alarm clock that in each minute rings for sixty seconds."

Walter Benjamin, "Surrealism," 1929

A dog with unresolved mysticism
has been chained to a window that looks
like an old mirror in a forest. Blank, yet

conspiratorial. And the young man
on the boulevard in Ottawa, the one
wearing a sepia t-shirt showing an even
younger Walter Benjamin, both men
are silently using their right hands to think
and smoke.
                There are many kinds of seduction
at play here. A one-act noir, barbaric, un-solitary
and sweet. Unbutton your shirt
and show everyone you've never

worn a bullet proof vest. You need
to spend some time among us: half
a day at least. Join us for the sushi
matinee, shoot some miniature toy
photographs, watch trees implode.

Sit on the park bench that's been
freshly dedicated to another's
undetectable and fugitive lifespan.

Take in an instantaneous onslaught
of family-friendly vertigo. Lean
toward the restive perceptions
of Gothic stained glass. Or follow
an interpretive trail of exile. Or refuse
to speculate, uncross your arms, refuse to gather
fruit, or like a promiscuous mermaid
learn how to swim.

It never
          stops, this haunting
never leaves, pareidolia, this tyrannical echo
that insists that what's on
          either
side of the psychogenic window is unfailingly
personal and also as completely communal
as a city sleeping through a night of rain. But who
can really say what someone else is thinking

as something more vague than hidden
          waits
for each of our monsters to come? The power's
just gone out. The city shivers and waits. Can you hand me
the flashlight in the cupboard above the stove? There. It's done, Lear

thanks me: resilient darkness makes us into mongrels and none
of this has ever belonged ... to anyone ← but, here's the thing: we really
must start to work damn hard to design a bot that can flag
the thanatos vs. eros quotient of any given post, weather forecast
or what's inside a person's careening life-span.

The Birds Now Suddenly Vanished

After C.D. Wright

1.

This life is the best you've ever been given.
The one you've been writing the moment you
started staring. Reading. Always removing.
There has never been a beginning to it ...
only what's moving across giddy eyelids
and across puffy daylight at dawn and daylight

                                        is what you've been given
                                                                                        when you wear
your riding
spurs to bed. I can't stop sleeping. Neither can I stop

insomnia's claws and I keep wondering   what if
time had the stamina to endure
as space does   what if

say, on May
18, in 1980 on this day across the whole world: only
two things take place, only two, *here* + *then* becoming
more immediate than *now*. I mean, metaphysics
aside, I dimly remember

when Mt. St. Helens blew the day apart in Washington, but I didn't know
then   how
                  lava covered

Harry Truman and his 16 cats, his perfect bourbon
and coke, his lodge on Spirit Lake ...
his 84 years—a former World War I pilot
and sometime later a bootlegger—and he refused
to leave the place he'd made his own. I have no

memory, none, that on the very same day

the Gwangju Massacre against 100s took place   a swirl
of gunfire into
students mostly and some workers, yes, women and men, yes
people across the ocean
from the state of Washington, the ocean made up
of ascending and descending waves,
forming beneath and inside
themselves. Imagine: two

things only, only two things
happening that day, the birds now

"However, bodies do not exist in space only, but also in time."

Gotthold Ephraim Lessing, *Laocoön*

suddenly vanished alongside Harry Truman
and his lake of drowning ginkgo trees.

The swirling ash pounding bullet holes into the ecology of a deranged
temporal architecture: students lying in straight lines
because that's how   they fell   when the bullets hit them. What
had they been studying to die this way? Oh, now

I get it: they
have to stay here
because what's in front of us

isn't what's
in front of us: the non-existing contradictions of
what the human heart finds itself

inside. The narrow
erupting, the singsong
memorial fountains. The juvenescent

decay. Nor can the unintelligible be left out.

2.

It's hard to recognize, but it was
here. They burned people here. A lot of people were burned
here. Says Simon Srbebnik, of Chelmno when, decades

after, he was filmed
there

by Claude Lanzman for *Shoah*. Who died, age 93, a little
more than 6 months ago. The film
maker, that is. And here's

3.

an 18th century Indian miniature
titled *Melancholy Girl with a Sitar*
and I don't even know
where the painting originally comes from, it's merely
a page on a calendar

we keep it on a window pane facing south
by Margaret the towering pea plant our son
brought home from a science experiment

at school. It's his job to remember
to water Margaret and change

the page of the calendar
each day. One image a day:

1 + 1 + 1 until we get to
this one: November
30, 2018.

A Friday. Each day succeeding in making what's (negatively) visible.

Here she is, the sitar seamstress
of unreleased melancholy

shining so ... she's shining
so ... the sky above her

a shimmering eggplant black
sea-lit with perfectly
restrained, exuberant
gold.

4.

This is necessary. To abandon
ourselves with what she's refused
to say, how everything
and nothing
                can be
stepped into and recast. Her sitar

containing almost only
what's past and gathered

into some future's insouciant
play. She's consciousness tethered
like a cable car
over a city at night in the mountains—

And someone has strewn Christmas lights
across a flat ravine of darkening snow—

5.

    But what you will never
see on November 30th
in 2018   or inside any calendar sold in stores   is a
date mostly forgotten: Etty
Hillesum's death

in 1943. It was a Tuesday.
Perhaps beneath a black sky
that may as well be omnipresent and fade-
away-less bluely
endorphin gold like the one
in the painting. Etty, who favoured
jasmine and who always returned to Rilke,
who may have tried to bring her memories
of Rilke to Auschwitz for who knows
how many days?

Her life's been caught in the penumbra
of its end. Her end made by Hitler.
And the release

of elegy—who can say what it's for, or means—let's be
blunt. We do know that something's smudged
between dolphins
speaking and the sound of pain happening

before memory's impact. We do know
that grief needs to
adjust itself to
what's inherited and to

be what's contagious. To discern
what's here. In *Andrei Rublev*, Tarkovsky spends only
seconds showing one woman braiding the hair of another
woman killed only minutes before in a cathedral how

can he know such things?

Homeric-Zen-Death Poem

A man who ran the Tokyo Marathon   owns a t-shirt given solely
to participants and now consider   the same man differently dressed
his hand waving a glow stick   with turquoise Hatsune Miku online
and what follows is a windy   apparition so terrifically windy
that everybody fails to walk   in a straight line while being recorded
by the camera the street cop   has to wear   all data shareable
and available on request   and afterwards there's a soothing
Himalayan cleansing lamp   to sleep beside when you're tired
if you must as you take in   what's in front of you
a raft with living cargo bobs   on the waves in the wine-dark

Aegean. Revive M = O/C   (where M is aesthetic value,
O is order and C is complexity)   and fly, little eons, fly: do we
can we still find ourselves among   time's obligatory creatures?

(Philippides as Athenian ghost the centuries have pulverized into neon
and kept running to 東京)

Or, how would a neuroscientist   studying evolutionary psychology
understand the sort of common   padlock sold in most bulk
grocery stores? How would   Martin Heidegger? Walker Evans?
Nan Goldin and the bodies   haunted by the wet and nomadic
light in her photographs?   And how to open what's locked?

*

Every day a 3 legged dog follows   me down to the ferry, no,
not that one, the one that goes   to Manitoulin Island
the dog's listening to the sounds   made by an untaught child
playing a piano in an empty school   the one beside the unfolding
beach and here's another   allegorical fact:

a few days or monads ago, I saw   a man holding a mirror
as he made his way along a brook   that kept arriving downstream
arriving from the bridal waterfall   that collects tourists. Eager.
Dignified. Down Syndrome.   His eyes stay straying, that man
who can go nowhere without his hand   mirror in his left hand

and his family who accompanies him   everyone careful on the slippery
rocks where (a fembot named   Basho sees) rollicking snails
and leopard frogs and audacious crawfish   summon their reborn
and invisibly finite lives   but cast inside this fearful and
runaway civilization who can say   what in the world

is contained   in a hand-held microphone?

An August Series

1.

of nomadic mannequins have been seeking
my inattentive eyes. There's always
something extra to learn. Something even
more beguiling than the surprised shadows
repetition makes: one luminous day

your lip muscles will be dissected by the word
deliberately, as in, who loves you deliberately
and whom do you love when last night
your easily distracted genitals were scanned
to make, then market, some fake ID? Not since
Doubting Thomas slammed a car door and invented
Industrial Rock have so many caged birds been set free
set alight in time's audioscape. Run.

2.

Hide. Tourists can juice their empathy engines
for real migrants by scrambling in the real Mexican
desert pretending to flee with a guide who won't
abandon them. An amazing thing to do, people
keep saying, giving it a Like. Like me, love everyone
and check it out: but instead of pine, actual coffins
holding those killed by gangs are made
from mango and elephant
ear trees.

Unpredictable,

and truly fundamental questions get posed far away

3.

from the nervous street.
Because the logistics of flight
patterns keep requesting a transient anatomy, a scrawl, don't
ever look up at night: science knows that every time
people rest their eyes in the competitive
heavens   another finite universe

splits apart ↔ quickening
the encoded and actual end
of this one →

Having Removed a Sliced Lemon from a Dutch Still Life

"To recognize a lemon in that lump of rubbery yellow there is to see the distinctive way this yellow occupies its space, holds and reflects the light, shades off in depth as its contours recede, to see how this yellow makes the inner substance surface, makes visible the pulpiness and the homogeneous sourness condensed there."

Alphonso Lingis, *The Imperative*

she placed it somewhere nearby
waited six invisible months
and its segments have now
become the amber of the lacquered
skin belonging to those damaged
people left inside the Neolithic bog
each a sacrifice left disinherited by
words

and
because they're growing children
who have stepped on a landmine need
their artificial limbs replaced every few months

Ω

the coral in the ocean   an auditorium of ghosts is   steadily shrinking inside
man-made zoological time   and who among us   expects the latest in desert
cyber warfare to be   a digital stampede of furious-Führer internet memes
did Bruno Ganz's fingers recognize   themselves   as each of them   came
alive   into the shape of a hand   a hand suddenly snared   with fingerprints
warming the frost on a fence   was anything left of the angel   as they were
transported inside what it means to live   consumed by shared and   yet
solitary forgetfulness

(For Bruno Ganz, 15.2.19)

trans – lay – shun

it's the waiting-in-line moments they remember best. strum, strum. how
does a normal even faceless person expand the range of what mediocrity

can be? hey it's mayhem in here better dodge those fish hooks strung from
wire the mind has left behind never being able to do stuff right is

the sort of thing you have to teach yourself like rope swallowing fire it's easy
to figure out just remind yourself your financial advisor's dreaming when she

says invest in tear gas or in countries selling coffee rugs made from stolen
giraffe meat ... hey! can't you ever say something nice? well everybody's

feeling pretty left out these finger nail sharpening days and what you call
being nice depends on who's looking ... but OK I know someone

in the market for a ¼ size violin and this someone's lovely in their bones and
that wasn't even tumbled or dictated by steep-roofed melancholy

or the remoteness of an aging that keeps trying to expand the range of what
bicycle poetry can be while performing in deepest Alpine Berlin   so be it

no one's gonna peep into your side-show genealogy even if I've only once
slept in a field ... your voice is beloved to me

Slow + Lettuce = Kale

or so says Kanzi the bonobo who
finds kale takes longer to chew than

lettuce does and he uses icons to speak what's solo
inside his mind raise hands please who knows

the surround sound

of seeing eye dogs being trained or who
is given to waiting out the nonstop night while

popping

some Toxic Waste candy with some castaway
furniture on the fully alive street curb waiting

for a piano to drop out of the unwired blue
sheer awesomeness is hidden sometimes much closer than you

think

j-u-b-i-l-e-s-c-e-n-c-e

in ready-made spring two geese hissing   their exhalations making a round
cloud of breath in the   chilled air   each breath a sphere the size
of a shrinking tennis ball   and a girl shoulders

a boy into some mud that sprays his licorice-coloured rubber boots   red
or black or undiscovered evaporeen   her sudden movement so smooth it
could be draped   over a kimono

stand at night   and passing overhead inside a plane   a tiny voice asking
her mother   are we in outer space   no   are we in Canada   not really
where are we   we're strewn across

classic YouTube   needing to feel welcome   do you know   have you seen
what skills you're passing on   to the next generation   from deep listening
within these idiopathic

night sweats   and with a responsibility to entertain   a dilapidated avant-
garde has leapt hidden and resilient like a sanctuary onto an embellished
and bare-bones table   and yes deep inside

each of us there's something that's always been beside itself   burrowing
something off-kilter omnivorous like a candle flickering in a fight sequence
something keeps us out of step with our

times like an anchor buried mid-drought   and keep trying kids   keep
trying to be attentive to what's actually h-a-p-p-e-n-i-n-g that
isn't the same as what's

÷
now

Sitting on a Bench on a Ferry Leaving Cortes Island, a Woman was Reading

this sentence *French gynecologists examining a ten-year-old girl found a wineglass*
from a dollhouse hiding in her cervix   she was reading a magazine to step
away

from the email she'd received while waiting in the car for the ferry   a man a
decent man who'd organized demonstrations   a man she'd spoken to only
weeks before was gone and while she was imagining a tiny plastic wineglass /
just then someone shouted

                                        a whale and there it was a

humpback breaching   am I really seeing this   it surges again
but it's her on the ferry that's deeply out of place now

the plane of reality has tilted   severely and brilliantly tilted   so that she's
swept off of the mind's deck   there's any number of humans sliding into the
ocean   swept aside and the waves are kingfisher blue ↔ grey and the world
is inside a kingfisher's untrammeled brain

and then she remembers the syringe she'd seen near Marine park
its muffled silence apart from the hot sand   a sharp its point sunk
into the huge log something hollow and utterly devoted   a full
grown syringe stuck in a bleached log   driftwood that's seashell white
and learning sign language   from a seascape that's becoming   deaf
before its time

Of These Things I'm Certain

Of These Things I'm Certain

Arthritis is having the teeth of a vampire
living inside. And mental

illness, as everyone knows, is endless
and rocking and the simple facts of many
disappearances. It's having to smoke
your fingers into the colour of cockroaches.
You can't quite picture the donut shop by yourself
someone needs to drive you there.
It's stop, and turn

toward yesterday's headlights. The sink, you can't
see yourself in the sink or any other surfaces.

It hurts to walk and the world's a space that finds you.
If it doesn't rain, if it doesn't rain. And then, just beyond

the gas station, it's truer than anything
that some
children
have chalked
a handful of stars on the sidewalk, a moon no one could believe in,
a cardboard truck, and incredibly

these words floating over everything
in simplest, impossible
blue: *We Know*

A Day's Desire Should Leave

1.

traces of itself like resin streaking
the air but children are being
forced into and then out of
their photographs   it took
                                        years but I quit smoking
not long enough ago and my eyebrows today
are suddenly disheveled like a deranged
and frenetic waiter and there's this
importunate
light

bulb somewhere over there that keeps at this open-mind-surgery
                                                                                                    first
the brain
is shaved and then body-wrapped in butcher's paper tick
                                                                                   tock
my idiot's dead and have you ever

2.

held
a bird's complete
body   its cells already
softening between flight
and gravity's gone
now   and then
to step
          inside what
the eye holds   the world's rim an edge   a deep myopia
of self-ruin deepening
where the present is a trap
          my very own nude
body a snare breathing time
beneath the bed in the head

a hologram
of need
and some thing's asleep in a cage
like eyes
perjured ↔ pillaged by drink
and endless

too for the first time
my inexplicably bruised
arms hand
cuffed behind my
back not the jade but
the normal kind resembling
nothing they're there to keep
me from self-harm (and nearby I'm
÷
this thinker
I admire but whose work
perplexes me
death is already
dissolving into a
companion because no
one will ever let it
remain indecisively) alone—

The Day I Went Grocery Shopping in the Dark I Didn't Know

After Edward Burtynsky & Sebastião Salgado

1.

I'd become a connoisseur and a witness
of impending old age. Unexpected power outage
in the supermarket. Darkness almost total but the store's
somehow still open ... you can't see what you came
to buy and so you go down a dark aisle with what your hands
manage to find and hold onto. Hesitant and
slow inside ... even the dark that's shuffling—

                    When someone's lifetime is finally weather-beaten
and unsafe, it's sent to Bangladesh where
men in hard hats slice it apart to salvage what chunks
they can. That's twelve somersaulting hours
ahead of local time here in the prairies. Work,
work, work.
                    A private tour of the factory demolition yards has cost me,
has set me back a few hundred demystifications, as reality loosens
starts to skid on blackening ice, wings it to one
of Saturn's disintegrating rings, and then capsizes.

                                                            Something's making
my mind betray itself. Words implode. Neural pathways
jump lanes ... the scale of which fills a swimming pool not
with insomnia, but the scandalous giggles of dandelion rot
and self-taught, self-decorating ink. And have I mentioned
that my mind's beginning to betray itself, beginning to
go. It's dwindling much faster than expected, passing through days
with the subtlety of sleeping asbestos. And in good
time, my world was slid into an MRI. The machine scanning
not a tailings pond, but my brain with blackened estuaries
on the screen the neurologist shows me. An MRI

finds the world in my mind's dwindling.   Its words like tufts
of cotton flaming out and gone into rain
rust, uncoupled mist and smoke.

Listen, they say: Look at people when they can hear you.

2.

When will I notice when I can't think anymore?

And how to prepare?

Can the mind enter itself

by making a joke while

wearing a Hazmat suit?

Or remember writing this poem?

The world tends to say no

to many seemingly puzzled things.

Everything lacking suitable

instructions.

Taking the first ferry,

with only two hours

sleep, my friend

with a camera, searching

↔

maybe this is what meaning is.

It takes so long:

finding only to lose one's loyalties.

*

One by one, each of them eventually said:
"I have a hard time separating."

The Sudden

darkness had her

make snow angels alongside
the train tracks then

repeat sing song to the wall pressed against
the rocking bed   and the rocking bed

had her lose her shit and
become crushed from the inside
out and then finally

climb into the future's
new nest   a fevered

bathtub made of charcoal and
stay there   stay there

all around   all around
unshareable surrender and
its soundless suspense

Everything Else is True

"In nature, everything is connected..."

David Suzuki, *The Legacy: An Elder's Vision for Our Sustainable Future*

1.

Incoherence being the thread that joins us.   We need to stare

from dot to imagined dot, even link up the ones
that have recently gone missing. Connect them like islands that vanish
before us. Look, let's sip some cough syrup
all night-and-every-day and join hands
on the Internet. Be together. Toggle back and forth and
close our eyes and see ... see what? See what's
missing
is all: there are

2.

mistaken holes of light foraging
                                        in the trees, I promise, someone keeps saying
to Socrates-as-Banksy. A can of spray paint caught in his hand. Thought-graffiti
as method. Finding what rhymes. What doesn't. Because history
keeps studying the ruins of stacked sleep. Not to forget
the helicopters shot down
                                        and burned blacker than crows
How long has it been since you played a game
of darts, removed a dart
from the bull's eye? Steadied the board? And reader: observe lite-little-lights
swishing along the arm in your brain as you read these very letters.
Once faced openly

[Ω]

an aging parable like-an-aging-brain eventually breaks down,

the parable's neurons eventually wondering: if a million
coloured marbles start rolling toward you at night
can you use the word demure in the same sentence
as you mention Jesus our Lord? But why would anyone choose
thoughts like that? There's absolutely nothing
in the body bag, nothing, insists the carpenter's remarkably friendly
computer software. The real problem is quickly becoming:
inside nano-evolutionary-technology everything else is
true, everything. And the world in atrophy begins
to acquire prosopagnosia—

3.

I can remember

the day Franz Kafka stood outside the U.S. embassy
holding a tooth brush and a bucket of Agent Orange. And
some kick-down-the-doors beeswax. In his hated
upon hated Praha. And a blinding bathtub

becoming conscious of the recently discovered
film footage of Moses just discovered
at Bikini Atoll. Copy that. Things forgotten
and things remembered, everything's connected ... every
thing ... and if no one can escape the hunger shaft, where are
we to go? Make an aircraft carrier into a life raft that's crammed
with the reincarnations of dead lemurs? Think of what's
narrowly sky and what lives there? Everybody:

drop what you're doing ↔ we're leaving. It's best that
the steel inside our cities remembers not us. It's like
watching a stampede of H.I.V. heading for some folks
in the 1980s. A ruin into people. A civilization
that's spent its whole life trying to perfect
the perfectly forgotten plunder or
well-meant mistake. Sometimes mistaking forceps

for precepts, a parable is a prelapsarian
colloquialism for: you're
not here for me. But keep trying. This is

4.

blessedness, this is an unraveling, a meandering double-exposure that cuts
its teeth reading Aleister Crowley and time
is an uneven 13 and my neighbour's
moon is made
from a syringe and a messy bowl: how could it be
otherwise? And oftentimes karma is infallible as satire
is a bitch. Next: dream slowly. Dream
safe. You don't

have to just lie there doing that. But what
if the floor you place your toes on in the morning is, you
know, high? Do you remember how to
                                        catch darts in your cupped hand?
It takes the mind to unscramble un-focus. To connect.
To be only a touchstone
for what's impeccable

even if you've never seen anything quite
like this: connect the long-awaited premiere of what's asleep
with what's inside
a deceased Mother's up-to-date
and playfully

needless and naturally insatiable species of wardrobe. Nature: gotta
love it when the oceanographer
played by Richard Dreyfus gets drunk
in the movie *Jaws*, his laughter
sounds like dolphins chattering—

Rare Sighting of a Guillotine on the Savannah

Some Things are Best Kept Quarantined

In words. For ninety days or more. Inside
a sonnet or traveling villanelle or. So that

what's happening inside chaos can be
studied safely. And once sequestered, observed.

Except: what crowds in to words leaks out. Weathers
the strange. A tincture of homecoming and ordnance.

I wish to be inside communication with you.
And: can you tell me what activity was your first love?

And: what government is flame resistant?
And: did you know that even sand is endangered?

And: out in the wild how badly beauty holds
time together as a child tries to regain the lost

        territory, lost years soldiers
        have taken from her. And

what if aging is the most unusual thing
people do with their bodies,

but hers is busy hauling vegetables in
plastic crates on skinny shoulders

in a sea of tents and a poet is an intern
for a non-profit that funnels anxiety

into hour glasses made not from disappearing sand
nor the displaced millions but remains on hand

when the daily cruise ships pull in. With its
endlessly shining and unusually affordable

Seaside View Café & Bar. And today's life
coach says: hunker down, you too can have abs

like someone who slices
fins off sharks for a living—

Both

Time should choose
a moment to camouflage
both. The jade

burial suit belonging
to the Han princess. And
the diabetic amputee
saying "excuse me"
as his wheel chair

jars the baby crying in
her 3-wheeled gargantuan
stroller. Darker than

surgeon green, more than two
thousand jade rectangles sewn

together with days
of ancient threaded gold. The insulin
pump attached to his belly with care.

Almost everywhere, trees
look at us but they can't see
the larger-than-life
vulnerabilities in
which we live. Our

slow burn. Neither
do we have before us
an illustrated history
of famous bridges all

of them built before tourists
would begin driving trucks
over terrorists to celebrate
TV. Nor even a reminder

of the old days when even
sacks of bottomless stars
begin to begin to wrinkle

inside memory's unswayable
and fist-dirt-dark obscurity.

And Right on Cue

1.

Everything's an unspooling fairy tale.

Take the Life-size silicon replica of a snowstorm
at dawn, the cringe-worthy Sumerian contact

sheets showing the future's zoo where the repository
of original extinctions

            is kept. Let's unplug
            the incubators. And

troll some Ponderosa pine. And the beautiful
robot on the diving board asks if you've noticed

that AI has been tracking every neural twitch, keeping

            an eye on how long you've stayed safe
            and sound in the perpetual scrutiny

of your favourite decade. What's implanted
inside tomorrow? Yes, no, or mebbe? Either
way → accelerate → either way → proliferate

today's just another randomly busy day to stay
galloping indoors   in the exponentially
                    redesigning
Anthropocene. It's what's confined behind reincarnated

2.

life number 3: the perfect contamination between nature's
restless eye and the unsteady man in the rain who is

forever without a 3-D printer. Our gargantuan
days persuade us to progress beyond each part
of ourselves less like birds flying suddenly away
from a bush than the easily forgotten particular:

that rattler we saw snaking across the lawn
during our vacation in Estuary, a prairie ghost
town, nothing

left of the homesteaders, their
abandoned bank only a concrete
vault on the prairie: a failure

of what resists as parched and incongruous
on the horizon as a head from Easter Island.

3.

A reality check rarely occasions a riot.

A woman who was with Anne Frank
when she died has just died herself,
95 years old in England.

Also, a reality check
rarely has side effects, even when
you try
to poke holes in the damn thing. Remember what
it feels like to walk not into a tailings

pond but a hotel lobby? Row upon row
of noggins of bad-boy and bad-girl bobble
heads for sale in the nearby gift shop,

and we`re all feeling pretty ugly right
now as we contemplate the new weekend,
discern the problems unique to ourselves
                                        and eavesdrop

4.

as rich folks walk
        barefoot on slate
                stepping stones
                        of the jungle boot camp, a resort that serves

Ayahuasca and offers freshly polished
sun helmets equipped with chic ear
buds, some tag along,
love-struck umbrellas.

        And right on cue, here's
        sound track thunder
        pretending to be Houdini
        in an escape room's
        entertainment coffin (there's

likely one to rent near you) and each
of us has once been our very own hinged

        and unhinged inaudible star. But who
        among us knows what it is that keeps
        us within its striking range, immediate
        and sure as tiger-lipped-sun falls on as

◘

No, that's not the way things happen, not at all: it's as un-lyrical as
simply this: 1 pit bull and 2 American Bullies coming
out of immediate
                Nowhere in the park by the lake, their leashes, their spittle
                flying, and
                                they want to kill

at least your dog. And only days later the shock recedes, one minute

the world's been wavery and brittle-clear, and in the next,
habit as narcosis returns, pervasive as
death rhyming with breath   never having missed a beat

Variations on the Words "To Decide" or: Still Life: Hope, B.C. August 23, 2009

After Aelbert Jansz van der Schoor & Willem Claesz Heda

After hiking in the mountains for a few days near Yoho, we decide to get a motel room. Have a shower together. Instead of pouring boiling water into dehydrated food pouches, eat at a Greek restaurant. It's been six weeks since you learned of your pregnancy. As we check in to the motel—chosen because you liked its variously coloured doors—two phones ring immediately—a friend of the owner's on his cell and a newspaper from Calgary on the land line—both calling to see if it was at Joseph's motel in which a fugitive accused of killing his wife in the States had hanged himself, the news breaking only moments before—

No, not in my motel, Joseph said.
Not here. Apparently,

the man wanted for murder
had once been

a contestant on a Reality-TV

show as a millionaire,
competing for a date:

his wife, a bathing suit model,
could only be identified
from the serial numbers

on her breast
implants—

The next morning I shuffle the advertising brochures in the office (butterfly farms, white water rafting, don't forget to visit Vancouver's aquarium, see its newly commissioned totem poles) while you complain about the bathtub's plugged drain and the noisy pipes in the next room. Joseph gives us a souvenir pen, tells us the names of his twin baby girls in the photograph, the ones whose mother had only just returned from Korea, and there she is, pushing the girls in a dual stroller at the far end of the parking lot.* The twins have a plastic slide, an orca seesaw and a small swimming pool beneath the sculpture of a squirrel peering around the deeply scored tree trunk, figures fashioned by a local artist who carves wood with a chain saw. We learn that Joseph visits Seoul once a year, stays for three weeks, takes in the ponies, some ballet, but is happiest here at home where he plays organ in a church most Sunday mornings.

Sunlight's making something move along the curtains. Only now a decade later do I remember

that each of the motel rooms was
named for a province. We stayed
in P.E.I.

that the Greek restaurant
had already closed
and the world is

the world is a more interesting place
with you always you inside
it—

---

*See the guide book *Vermeer, Rembrandt and the Golden Age of Dutch Art: Masterpieces from the Rijksmuseum* (an exhibition which showed in the Vancouver Art Gallery May 10-September 13, 2009) for a few of the generic conventions Aelbert Jansz van der Schoor and Willem Claesz Heda most likely kept in the back of their heads when they were working on canvases that eventually ended up only a few canals from where the Nazis forced the Jewish Council to do their bidding, Dutch still life painting embodying a coded realism that, requiring the subtlest of perception and refulgent skill, names the disaster of an allegorical mortality. Finally, it has to be

that you can pick everything up in your hands . . . not only with your eye: a luring vanitas must offset the artificial with peripheral vision's spontaneity and exactitude.

Rare Sighting of a Guillotine on the Savannah

"It is not my intention to make anything comprehensible. I am of the opinion that there are sufficient paintings which one understands after a shorter or longer delay, and that therefore, some incomprehensible paintings would be welcome."

René Magritte

1.

When I lived on the savannah,   alpine scenes invited
themselves inside and soon   sold almost everything off,
leaving me an under-age   TV remote on the explosion
-proof table, the hand-painted   one a class of children
had made for a charity auction.   Grandmothers in Africa.
When I lived in the forest,   there was a chess set waiting
all night by the window: one of the kings was Napoleon
straight across from Stalin   and Stalin he's shaking hands
with Pandora, and you can hear   him saying: *You're not*
going to like this, devotchka,   *but my face has finally*
disappeared beneath yours—   *Damnatio memoriae*: something

even more personal than being   robbed while hitchhiking.

2.

Despite it being too early,   the cafeteria menu is diplomatic:
the fun's over: you better eat   as fast as you can. Longing

3.

for a meaningful existence
the hospital bed shrank in winter
doused itself with aviation fuel
awaits the high-resolution
sunrise

4.

often mistaken for second   generation ice-age art,
the next century has become   an explosive splinter-verse,
an outbreak of baroque   hardship. When I lived
in the ready-made forest,   alpine scenes like waterlogged
papyrus predicted the unknown   instability of clouds,
seasons made from old horoscopes   and DNA stumbling
through some kind of recessive   and derelict choreography.
Thinking on a planetary scale,   inside rain's intensifying
October, there's something   pushing all the way
through us as if we're not even   here and where are those

vaccines you said you'd send via

5.

the open-hearted drone? The one you
control with what's left of
what's Neanderthal
that's lost inside
the mind's
trick
of
↔
impersonating itself:
thought being like a dog straying
across the edgeless

(But each minute has a separate brain, Brenda Hillman *once* protested)

at once story-less and rapt, but
don't worry. Things usually go away.
The *Smilodon fatalis* is gone and today's
deer see blue more thoroughly than we do.

Words Were Never Ours to Keep

Words once awoke as the very first window
to light the dark each morning across the alley

an opening in an autobiography of sorts
though each time we kept missing that words

aren't ours have never been ours to keep
words are the first hand-held axe gaming

itself into a GPS with no help from us
and now we've been left with just under

three hundred varieties of having little to say
the ocean's ghost nets having quickly

so slowly become the finest prose writers
of these archaeopteryx widening →

and palpably Invisible
spindle drift times ←

Obsessions are Evidence

"of the contradiction between the ego and the world. To remove the splinter from the mind, to give respite to this relentless dripping which never ceases, the need to satisfy the urge increases."

Enrica Viganò, curator of *W. Eugene Smith: A Retrospective*, Martin-Gropius-Bau, 2011

You had to have been there: Living in the old paradigm—
the scientist trying to isolate what makes obsession—

*

he stuffs the barn owl into a tube that keeps
its wings snug and then moves electrodes in its wide
awake brain looking for clues + the video footage
smuggling spectacular moments in World History—
the instant a young fan shows Gene Simmons
his actual vampire face tattooed down there between
her thighs his mouth caught in a wonky smile
or choose to scramble the 140 mile race in the Sahara
(Amy Palmiero-Winters aged 46 her prosthetic left leg
becoming stuck beneath a rocky outcropping)
relentless the Marathon des Sables you keep having
to be here—always leaving LEAVE BRITTANY ALONE—
there are sanctions huddled in every paradigm
but what if pluralist time became both desert bright
and matrilineal and here comes someone older
much older wearing a Joseph Beuys life jacket and is

a creative with an appetite for disorder

*

When one considers evil, human possibility, chance, and the durability of the self under horrendous conditions, the Holocaust exists as a kind of relentless limit case for all thought.[1]

---

[1]It is an open question as to whether the Holocaust has been relegated to being perceived generally as a past event characterizing the worst of the twentieth century, rather than an ongoing problem and crisis that refuses to be resolved. This treatise cannot begin to sketch out the intricacies of this issue, though I will point out two approaches that acknowledge the necessity of regarding the Holocaust as something that intrudes upon contemporary thought and experience: in *Radical Evil: A Philosophical Interrogation*, Richard J. Bernstein evaluates ethical theory—from Kant to Levinas—by challenging it to account for Auschwitz; Ben Taub, describing the plight of sub-Saharan refugees in their attempts to emigrate to Europe, refers to how "the German embassy in Niger sent a cable to Berlin . . . comparing the conditions in Libya's migrant connection houses to those of Nazi concentration camps. Sometimes the sick are buried alive" (43). Both writers imply that the Holocaust indicts our seemingly endless capacity for indifference to the pain of others. What would it mean to be the civil servant who read this cable in Berlin and then looked south out of a window in the Reichstag in the direction of Paul Eisenman's Memorial to the Murdered Jews of Europe a few streets away?(Not to forget that Gene Simmons, the bass player for the band KISS, performs beneath the band's name in lights, the letters SS using the Nazi *sig* rune that represents a forked lightning stroke. The group is playing in Leipzig, Munich and Vienna as part of their Farewell Tour that begins later this month.)

Evolutionary Game Theorists Propose

That ear-worms made from birdsong, combined with the Prisoner's Dilemma, clenched teeth and clumsy fists, eventually gave our ancestors their skill for denial. Something that sleeps like dormant and degraded snow within their descendants → Forget →

the untried woman growing cucumbers

and listening to Buddhist talk

radio, a septuagenarian who once gave a hand to

Pol Pot make several million deaths occur. This was

in Cambodia in the same year David Bowie

composed *Warszawa* after going for a walk

during a layover on a train trip heading towards

Moscow through the sleet and desolation

all kinds of people had made of Poland.

And back then I was fine

tuning my taste for all kinds of oracular drugs. Listening

to Tubular Bells in a blizzard and leaning into clocks

made for retroactively singing Just Because, nobody

on our small town street (but the war vet) knowing

much about anywhere. There should have

been, there should be a word

to contain whether we recognize

or not what's far away

◘

Not knowing where to go after their childhoods, decades quickly get purged of everything except a handful of leftover facts. Oblivion: a spectral arboretum growing cruelty out of derisive and accelerating stone

Beginner's Zazen

—not aiming for the perfect breath just one that's good
enough and then perhaps another that follows
                                        when thoughts of a bathtub alight
with gasoline   something rogue   something coming
from behind my right shoulder   an image there in the cloudy
north   and then I let it go   these things just
happen: knowable = and ≠ unknowable

... merely a flock of hurrying
hurrying close by ... one breath that's simply good
enough   the capricious mind is merely ordinary
is merely to be acknowledged   because another mind lives underneath
call it a forgotten well during continual rain-light ... call it
                                        something precise spelled as vigilant
                                        that's always been watching beneath the eyes →

*

And then the door bell rang   two days ago   and there's a beggar who
weeps mostly in another language but we have no grass for him to cut

and if he's just given something to make him go away
will he return and return
and return to this door again   this door that closes against him?

              Turned away   the man rearranged his face   composed
and hurled himself away on his bicycle   an old machine that rends
itself past   darkening drift-light:

a misery: a severing of care: whatever denial is. Come back   I say to him now

"Filled with shame, Shariputra and Mokuren had a vision of the precariousness of life. They understood it to be a torrent that carries beings to the shores of death in less time than it takes to realize we're being swept along, with hardly time to find safety from the deluge."

Taisen Deshimaru, *Mushotoku Mind*

though he's long gone from our expensive street
accompanied by green-feathered overarching elms   and a brand new
rock garden in the front yard   my wife has made   the yard a sleep
of deepening soil into which over a hundred nascent plants have
been carefully introduced only this past week   come back

I repeat I want
to put unfinished money in your hand ↔ look

in your eyes and give you more than you expect
and then ask you to destroy
my aching desire to be seen   mollify my fear that I could
become as you are

‰

Amongst the guilty privations of Things.
...
a perverse reclamation a poetry
of sorts   shouldering
the cowardice in failure the failure
that's riveted to cowardice—

A Seventh Sense

Récriture

—1969 Moon Landing ... Flash Forward—

To online emotional escorts chanting *Dies Irae.*
Flash forward to the present when kids these days
would far rather be a famous YouTuber
than any astronaut. Not to forget the increase
in verbally- transmitted diseases.

—And what's to see & listen to is written by committee—

On your left the ocean named empathy
and on your right some hotels famous
for making your mind oblivious to money

and in between somebody naked running down
the tranquil and disfigured beach
it's a curse of some kind

this ... our octave range ... it's not as though
the garbage tanker alight with the most beautiful
flame has come from nowhere ... now has
it?

—is there any way faster to shut down a pyjama party?—

Well, yes, A conquistador's gold. We can live through
this can you? the Amazon brain wants to know asleep
all beneath the moon's orange duvet as bulldozers rip
and saws clear-cut and bull pizzles piss
everything way past the tipping point →

—Mad Meg's on a shoplifting spree plunders the malls of hell—

Prequel becoming sequel

"Bolsanaro's policy [of deforestation] is the equivalent of adding , if just for a year, a whole second China to the planet's fossil fuel problem—and on top of that, a whole second United States."

David Wallace-Wells, *The Uninhabitable Earth*

"The language of citation [Antoine] Compagnon appropriately calls it récriture—has found a new lease of life in our own information age."

Marjorie Perloff, *Unoriginal Genius: Poetry by Other Means in the New Century*

"One morning in the middle of April, 1943, Ken told me about a London radio broadcast, made the day before, by General Sikorski, the Polish prime minister in exile, who was appealing to Poles in Poland to support the ongoing uprising in the Warsaw ghetto. The ghetto was systematically being annihilated. Sikorski said—Ken spoke slowly—that 'The greatest crime in the history of mankind is taking place.'

Only during moments of forgetfulness, when thinking about nothing, did the enormity of what was happening make itself felt. The enormity was then present in the air, under the spring sky, addressing a seventh sense which I still cannot name."

John Berger, "Kraków"

Zen and a Dinosaur

A Thought Experiment

As I type, my fingertips are waxy white with Raynaud's syndrome, the result of aging, anxiety and winter blurred together. This early a.m. was our first real snow this year. There are so many species of time.

Imagine Marcel Proust coming upon these sentences from *War and Peace* for the first time:

"and, stepping off the ferry, [Prince Andrei] looked at the sky Pierre had pointed to, and for the first time since Austerlitz saw that high, eternal sky he had seen as he lay on the battlefield, and something long asleep, something that was best in him, suddenly awakened joyful and young in his soul. This feeling disappeared as soon as Prince Andrei re-entered the habitual conditions of life, but he knew that this feeling, which he did not know how to develop, lived in him."

You can almost taste the joy Proust must have found in this recently deceased writer (who lived briefly in the twentieth century alongside the world Proust knew).

And if Tolstoy were to be given *In Search of Lost Time*, he would see how his passage had metamorphosed into Proust's masterpiece like the game Japanese people play when they place small pieces of paper in water that then eventually twist and unfold to become flowers or houses or people. Prince Andrei as involuntary memory.

But what if Proust had been born in the twentieth century and, in 1966 found himself reading Jean Améry on Auschwitz: "In other words, nowhere else in the world did reality have as much effective power as in the camp, nowhere else was reality more real." To think of Proust reading Améry before he set out to write *In Search of Lost Time* is to summon an emotion that melds nausea with intense curiosity. As twenty-first-century readers, we have an imperative to do so.

Zen and a Dinosaur

Home is what travels through us.

*

Jakob, my youngest son, had just come upstairs to show me a drawing he'd made of a shark. When he's not drawing he's writing, fan fiction mostly, though he wouldn't call it that. And he knows all sorts of statistics regarding the bite force of the various apex carnivores that populate his stories. After we spoke about the shark, which was actually a hybrid between a Great White and a vampire—the fins are folded across the shark's chest like Dracula asleep in his coffin—I returned to what I'd been reading: Janwillem van de Wetering's *The Empty Mirror*, a memoir of the time he'd spent in a Zen monastery in Kyoto as a young man. The book had recently arrived in the mail from Amazon, but the first time I'd read it was about a year after it was published in 1973. I'd borrowed it from the public library in New Hamburg, the small town in southern Ontario where I grew up.

*

I've decided to approach Buddhism again because a counselor has suggested I take some meditation classes to see if they'll help with my steadily increasing anxiety. Medication doesn't seem to be doing much anymore. And I continuously stumble with cognitive therapy.

After years of worsening short term memory problems, insomnia, and seemingly insurmountable anxiety, I've finally seen a neuro-psychologist who gave me an extensive series of tests that resulted in a diagnosis of NVLD (nonverbal learning disability), something he explained to me as being "a developmentally-based disorder that is often associated with deficits in nonverbal communication and perception." Apparently, I've "historically compensated" for these weaknesses by relying on verbal skills. People with NVLD are often clumsy, and find spatial learning difficult. We experience acute anxiety, inexplicable mood shifts, and find it hard to "adjust" to social difficulties. Given to obsession, we also consider the environment to be intrinsically threatening. We're susceptible to depression and are prone to substance abuse. Little is known about the disability because it's only recently been acknowledged, but it's theorized that it might grow more intense as one ages.

*

While there are parts of the Van de Wetering memoir I remember, there was nothing familiar about the particular scene I'd been reading when Jakob came into the room: he was trying to control his anger after being rebuked by a master while working in the monastery's garden. What's impossible for me to grasp is that, between my first and second time encountering the sentences in this book, more than forty years have passed. What I'd like to know now is what my younger self would think if he'd been able to look up from the library book in his hands and have loose access to the man he'd somehow become. If I could have him shift from that long gone, fraying chair (that went to his bedroom because it was no longer needed by a deteriorating grandparent) to the one in this room in Saskatchewan, a chair that came from IKEA, what would he think?

After doing a quick mental probe, he'd immediately ascertain that he hadn't become enlightened. How was this possible? What had interfered with those plans to emulate Van de Wetering and go to Japan immediately after completing high school and stay there until achieving satori, something that, according to the memoir, the young Dutch man had (inexplicably) failed to accomplish? But before he, the younger me that is, could register disappointment in his spiritual state, remove the bad taste from his mouth, he would have to take in that he'd become a father, and did the child's very long, blond hair mean that his mother was Scandinavian?

Looking around the busy sunroom, this younger self would see that books have remained important. There are hundreds of them, in shelves and piled on the floor. Literature (poetry mostly), others on ecology, art history, philosophy, five or six concerning addiction, and an entire bookcase devoted to the Holocaust. Art postcards on the walls, binoculars on the desk facing a wall of windows, and a large photograph of a woman's bare feet with the words *welcome home* painted on her toes. A stationary bicycle. Oddly, a few Polaroids. That both rooms are painted the same yellow is uncanny (not that he'd use this word): on the one hand, it feels exactly right, but, on the other, it's slightly disturbing: don't one's tastes change or develop over time?

Instead of the large, classical Buddha statue he'd once owned, there's a very small one almost entirely obscured by a tarantula fern. Also a small Bodhisattva, painted with what appears to be pink nail polish. No plastic milk carton storing LP records. And what's with the antique dolls? A half of a lemon that seems mummified nestled beside a cactus, and stranger still, a few things inside Ziploc bags taped against a wall: what's left of a flower (he wouldn't know it's a five-year-old souvenir from an evening stroll down Nieuwe Keizersgracht in Amsterdam); the darkening claws of a bird that once struck a window. A finely detailed toy camel has been cut in half in its middle, and both parts glued to the wall. If you look at the back part of its torso, it appears as if the animal has exited from the house, but at the same time, only a finger's width away, the neck and head, forefeet in mid stride have just emerged seemingly from another dimension on the other side of the wall and entered the room again.

And yes, there it is: what's now a very old scar, left over from when, only the week before the teenager had started reading the Van de Wetering, he'd lit a match and watched it burn out on the skin of his left hand. There are other scars about whose origin he won't know. There was no Internet when he was in *his / my* early twenties so he had to discover cutting on his own. There once had been a few case cutters left over from working nights in a grocery store.

*

The teenager's Buddha statue only exists in the photograph to my left, an image showing a slightly shattered statue in an open suitcase. My father was de-cluttering and he decided to bring me the statue that I'd stored with him, but, silly man, he packed it with socks and underwear, and then had it go thru *normal luggage* on a flight from Ontario to here about 5 years ago. Now there's a concrete instance of the transitory nature of reality. To me, the photo is a finely compressed detail that speaks of Dad slowing down, being inattentive and the picture is also a nicely goofy setting for this statue, one that could even stimulate its own koan: instead of concentrating on the face you had before you were born, hold the thought of a fairly shattered Buddha in a suitcase along with the socks and underwear of a 76 year-old and see what this tells you about emptiness and its vicissitudes.

*

Wikipedia tells me that Van de Wetering died over a decade ago, as a man nearing eighty in 2008. After publishing the book on Zen in the 1970s, he'd made a career writing detective fiction, eventually leaving the Netherlands for the States, though he did revisit his youthful sojourn in Kyoto, turning out another memoir in 1999, this one called *Afterzen*. From it, and an interview online, I've learned that one of the reasons he initially turned to Zen was his confusion over suffering and evil: only after the war did he learn that the teenage boys who had disappeared from his school in Rotterdam had died at Treblinka. I also learned that booze had been a decades-long companion until his wife had put her foot down. When I'd originally read Van de Wetering, he was in his early 40s, and he had over thirty books yet to write. Apparently, he'd maintained his meditation practice more or less and did it in the proximity of a small altar he'd made, decorating it with Dutch sea shells to remind him of his childhood and also some plastic dinosaurs to keep the idea of extinction directly in front of him. I've never gotten much out of detective fiction, but I'm half tempted to order one of his mystery novels. Someone who decorates a home-made altar with a toy dinosaur is likely to be good at nestling surprising details inside his fiction: small gems that coalesce around how the world appears perhaps only to him.

*

A red-breasted nuthatch has just flown off with a sunflower seed from the feeder two stories below. I put out seeds all year, even during the summer. The bird may be the one who waits for me in the early morning when I replenish the feeder. Often we'll look at each other, only an arm's length apart. Almost all birds appeal to me, but I've wondered for years why this specific species gives me a particular dopamine rush. It's precognitive: as soon as I even remotely register the grey blue feathers of the bird, its eye stripe and black beak, it seems as though my hypothalamus is flooded with not only simple equanimity, but euphoria as well. For years now, I've wondered why one of these small creatures triggers these emotions. I'm unsure, but through meditation practice, I think that I may be getting closer to the cause. Feelings are so bizarre. If they seem to arrive as contemporaries of the present, a reaction to immediate circumstances, they may in fact be very ancient, far older than anything we can consciously identify.

I'm lousy at meditating and suspect that decades of anxiety (among other things), have torpedoed the tissues in my brain ... but here's the thing: back when I was reading *The Empty Mirror* and planning on going to Kyoto, I used to take long winter walks along a nearby frozen river, hike through the forest that followed its contours. Recently, during sessions of regular, extraordinarily difficult, breathing exercises, I've found that unusual images suddenly veer toward my unanchored mind, some bizarre—Michael Jackson's face during plastic surgery shot by on one occasion—but other images seem to arrive from my own deep past, showing memories that have been lost for decades. Sitting on a dock as a child about to try water skiing for the first time, the waves making my feet move up and down, everything as if filmed by a parent, but ordinary people didn't have the technology to record anything back then like we do now. Gene Simmons spitting blood on a stage from the one time I saw KISS. Eventually, a recollection from one of those walks along the forest by the river came into view. In it, snow is everywhere, deeper than my knees and thick tufts of it are on the trees. In this memory, I watch myself stop walking and turn around to look behind. There's a bit of snow falling from some kind of pine tree. A grey sky. I can't say for certain, but upon repeated viewings of this scene when I've been observing breaths for a half hour or so, I've wondered whether I didn't turn around because I heard the singular sound that a long dead white-breasted nuthatch once might have made. And within that sound, I felt a sense of well-being that nestled somewhere inside and then seemingly vanished beneath the subsequent decades that happened next. I'll never know for certain if there actually was a nuthatch (though I do know that I have to struggle to keep references to snow out of the poetry I write). And I know that birds aren't here to provide us with spiritual sustenance. It's simply that some things went right in my life after those moment in the snow, many things went right, and some other, different things began to occur very shortly after reading van de Wetering, some habits began that distracted me from the ambition to travel to Japan.

*

But what's staying with me now is a detail of which I have no recollection in Van de Wetering's story. The ship that took him to Japan docked briefly in Bombay where he went ashore to be surrounded by beggars, their number surprising him. "The hunger we knew in Holland during the winter of 1944/45," he says, "seemed to be a normal and permanent phenomenon here [in Bombay]." While there, a sailor told him that there was a brothel where women were kept in cages and to his credit, van de Wetering caustically asks whether it would make any difference to either the beggars or these women whether a clever young man managed to gain enlightenment after spending a year or so in a monastery. I note that he doesn't call these caged sex workers *prostitutes* but the Dutch word translated into English tells me that he thought of these people as *women*. I don't have the slightest inkling of what this passage meant to me when I first read it. Van de Wetering had these temporary misgivings in 1958, en route to Kyoto, and eventually I read and then forgot about them during the 1970s, but today, I can't help but wonder whether any of these people, peripheral to the memoir, are still alive today, more than sixty years after that stop in Bombay.

Imagine the trajectory of their lives. If we're honest, we'll admit we can't. To ask what happened to *only one* of the beggars that Van de Wetering saw, or stood next to, is to recognize the vastness of oblivion and that almost all human experience is evanescent and cruelly unknowable. I don't know how to confront this fact, except to put it like this: while I was burning incense, reading *The Empty Mirror* for the first time, listening to Deep Purple's *Machine Head*, and going for walks in the snow, I had no idea that the Khmer Rouge was beginning its policy of genocide in Cambodia.

Contained in a heavy cardboard box, Ben Kiernan's history of the Pol Pot regime has recently arrived, and this is one of the books my previous self would have noticed if I'd been able to transport him from the first reading of van de Wetering to the second. But I have no sense as to what reading the Kiernan will actually mean when I finally find the time to start the book. I've been to Auschwitz, Mauthausen, Westerbork and Dachau. I'm fairly certain that I'll never go to Cambodia's killing fields.

*

Time baffles me. I simply cannot understand how one day passes into another one. For years now, I've thought that time is the most mysterious of our experiences, but now I understand that being a parent means having to acknowledge something even more perplexing than whatever time is: to bring a birth is also to bring one more death into the world.

*

According to Armstrong™ (Canada's Premiere Bird Food), its product named *Persistence* (a blend of quality seeds, nuts and dried fruits, including pineapple) is "wild bird food for woodpeckers, nuthatches and other *hardworking birds* (my emphasis). Neoliberalism in bed with John Calvin.

*

A few facts and questions that must interrupt this essay:

1. My blond son's mother isn't Scandinavian; her heritage is Ashkenazi.

2. When I was a child I could make snow forts out of what was left after a plow went down the road, and these forts would be higher than my father. My sister (who still lives in the area) tells me that there's rarely any snow on the hills where we used to go tobogganing all winter. It rains more than it snows. She puts this down to global warming.

3. Before this past early spring, a catbird had never visited our backyard, but today, one has. Using my binoculars, I follow this new arrival as it searches for seeds ... the black, grey and red on his body summon something deeper than ink, a sky of the thickest rain, and a piece of red felt that's rarely seen.

4. Jakob has two large overflowing plastic boxes of dinosaurs tumbled in disarray. Each toy a perfect replica of a specific species. A large collection of plastic toys that have been made of polymers that have made the long journey from China to his bedroom.

5. Jakob doesn't know about refugees dying in the Sahara or children walking from Guatemala to the United States, but one day he'll be forced to confront the reality that while he's been writing stories about dinosaurs, Joy the murderous Clown, and also before, when he was teaching himself how to draw by creating hybrid sharks, another extinction has been happening—in the oceans and rain forests that are so far from the Canadian prairies; and everywhere else too, including Saskatchewan's grasslands—and there's nothing he can do about it. Extinction is a word no one can accurately understand: it may be

an indifferent volcano; we might force ourselves to its rim, but who has the courage to look down into what's beyond the edge?

6. Will Jakob know food insecurity in his old age as Van de Wetering experienced in his childhood?

7. How will he eventually remember the climate strikes we went to when he was eight, nine and ten?

8. Can anyone doubt that our children will look back on us with incomprehension and likely a long abiding sense of contempt?

9. Dinosaurs once were real and knew nothing of us, and we've put them in movies and museums, but what's most important today is that together we've made fossil fuels.

Notes

"My Single Life-time in Exchange for a Burst"

David Buckel was a LGBT lawyer who immolated himself in 2018 to protest inaction on global warming.

"Three Minds"

The notion that the mind is something surprised by space is indebted to David Abram's *The Spell of the Sensuous*. The description of samurai wars is from *Japanese Death Poems: Written by Zen Monks and Haiku Poets on the Verge of Death*. Ed. Yoel Hoffmann.

"The Birds Now Suddenly Vanished"

A description of Harry Truman can be found easily online.

The information about the Gwangju massacre is from *Human Acts* by Han Kang. The line "Nor shall the unintelligible be left out" is from C.D. Wright's poem "My American Scrawl."

Etty Hillesum wrote diaries and letters extending from 1941-1943. She managed in this work to embody the perplexities facing a young, ambitious writer who gradually came to understand that, as a Jewish woman living under Nazi-controlled Holland, she was unlikely to survive the war. Astutely perceptive of the psychologies of both victims and perpetrators, perhaps owing to her own depressive mood disorders, she wrote from within the chaos imposed by the Nazis, refused to go into hiding, and eventually perished at Auschwitz-Birkenau.

"Homeric-Zen-Death Poem"

Hatsune Miku is a female anthropomorph with long, turquoise hair who performs in concerts, The equation M = O/C is taken from Ferris Jabr's "Beauty of the Beasts," *The New York Times Magazine*. January 13, 2019. 22-33 +48. 東京 is Japanese for Tokyo.

"An August Series"

The detail about coffins made from mango trees is derived from Óscar Martínez, *A History of Violence: Living and Dying in Central America*.

"Having Removed a Sliced Lemon from a Dutch Still Life"

For information on children who have lost limbs to landmines, see David D. Kirkpatrick, "Hidden Calamity In Yemen's Civil War,: A Million Land Mines," *The New York Times*, February 17, 2019, 1 + 14. For information on Bruno Ganz, see Anita Gates, "Bruno Ganz, 77, Actor Who Played an Angel and Hitler, is Dead," February 17, 2019, 27.

"Obsessions are Evidence"

The reference to Gene Simmons being taken aback by a fan's tattoo is from *Time Magazine*, November 2, 1998. 63. The reference to the long distance race in the Sahara is from Jeré Longman "An Amputee in the Sahara," *The New York Times, Sports*, April 28, 2019, 1+ 6-8. Go to YouTube for "Leave Brittany Alone" (2011). For the reference to migrants, see Ben Taub "We Have No Choice." *The New Yorker*. April 10, 2017. 36-49.

"Evolutionary Game Theorists Propose"

For information pertaining to Grandma Chaem, see Julia Wallace, "A Cambodian's Bucolic Life, Charges of Atrocities Aside," *The New York Times* (Sunday, February 26, 2017) A6.

"Slow + Lettuce = Kale"

To learn more about Kanzi, who lives at the Ape Cognition and Conservation Initiative in Des Moines, see Jeffrey Kluger, *The Animal Mind*. Special *TIME* Edition (Spring 2019).

"Sitting on a Bench on a Ferry Leaving Corts Island, a Woman was Reading"

The sentence about the wineglass comes from "Findings," *Harpers* May 2018, 96.

"j-u-b-i-l-e-s-c-e-n-c-e"

Evaporene is a word I've invented.

"Some Things are Best Kept Quarantined"

The reference to sand disappearing is from David Owen, "The End of Sand," *The New Yorker*, May 29, 2017, 28-33.

"A Rare Sighting of a Guillotine on the Savannah"

See Brenda Hillman "Chicago Black Friday Protest Near Apple," and for the information regarding the vision of deer, see Mark Doty, *The Art of Description: World into Word*.

"A Seventh Sense"

The allusion to Mad Meg is to Bruegel's painting *Dulle Griet* (1562), which can be found in the Museum Mayer von den Bergh, Antwerp. Of this painting, Christian Vöhringer writes: "a saying has [Mad Meg] `plundering the maws of hell,' that is profiting from the downfall of others" in *Pieter Bruegel 1525/30—1569*.

"Thought Experiment"

The reference to the game Japanese people play with small pieces of paper is taken from *In Search of Lost Time*, Vol. 1.

Acknowledgments

This collection has been composed over some difficult years. Without the ongoing support of Amy Snider, my partner, and my children, Andy, Jesse and Jakob, I wouldn't have been able to complete the book. This book is dedicated to them. And I dedicate the book to birds everywhere.

Friends over the years have offered encouragement and advice. Derek Brown, Jeremy Desjarlais, Paul Endo, gillian Harding-Russell, Randy Lundy, Craig Melhoff, Ben Salloum, Jeremy Stewart, Dan Tysdal—your friendship means much. Also thanks to the members of the poetry workshop group *POV* (Jes Battis, Troni Grande-Sherbert, Tracy Hamon, Medrie Purdham, Melanie Schnell, Tara Solheim and Kathleen Wall) who helped make the poems cleaner. Susan Lohafer, likely the best reader I know, and whose own work inspires mine, has buoyed my spirit for decades. Philip Charrier deserves a special note of thanks: his willingness to read all of my work and his perfect advice for writing creative non-fiction means that this collection couldn't have been written without him. Not to forget his extraordinary skill as a photographer—his capacity for surprising composition has helped me see the world with greater intricacy.

Decades of teaching at the University of Regina have allowed me to interact with many wonderful students, too numerous to name individually. I would, though, like to offer thanks to Joel Blechinger, Jesse Desjarlais, and Sarah Fahie for their thoughtful, indeed sparkling emails and helpful reading recommendations. The English Department's willingness to allow instructors to develop their own idiosyncratic courses has enabled me to combine teaching with research and writing.

I also wish to thank Jim Johnstone; it is literally true that this book wouldn't exist without his steady, generous support and excellent guidance. My very deep thanks go to him. Also, many thanks to Erica Smith who somehow managed to make wonky lines fit onto the page.

Some of the material in this collection has appeared in different forms in the following journals and presses: The Alfred Gustav Press, *CV2*, *Queen's Quarterly*, and *Transition*. My thanks to the editors for permission to reprint this work.

Michael Trussler lives in Regina, Saskatchewan. He writes poetry, short stories, creative non-fiction and literary criticism. An amateur photographer, he also has a fascination with visual art. His writing has won numerous prizes and has been anthologized domestically and internationally. He teaches courses in creative writing, literary theory and contemporary literature at the University of Regina.